HAS ANYONE
SEEN MY
FATHER?

HAS ANYONE SEEN MY FATHER?

Marion Daniel

New Wine Press

New Wine Ministries
PO Box 17
Chichester
West Sussex
United Kingdom
PO19 2AW

ISBN 978-1-905991-12-9

Typeset by CRB Associates, Reepham, Norfolk
Cover design by CCD, www.ccdgroup.co.uk
Printed in Malta

CONTENTS

ACKNOWLEDGEMENTS

Thanks, Popsy, for all my lovely cuddles growing up and the soft look in your blue eyes after I'd been disciplined. By the way, I've forgiven you for not giving me the 40 shillings for roller skates when I burst in on you at work and asked you to be quick 'cos they might be sold!

Thank you, heavenly Father, for the freedom in my soul that my father has imparted to me to write this book from a place of victory.

My sincere thanks to all my Sozo family who have made this book possible through your love and commitment to the Lord and myself and the vision we are called to. Bless you all.

Marion

CONTACT
INFORMATION

Postal address:
Sozo Ministries International
Sozo House, Alma Road, Romsey
Hampshire SO51 8ED, United Kingdom

Telephone: 01794 522511 *Fax*: 01794 522577
Email: email@sozo.org *Website*: www.sozo.org

INTRODUCTION

Most people would agree that fathers hold a unique place in family life. Whilst every child has a special bond with his/her mother – the person who bore them into the world – a child's relationship with their father is different in many ways. Whether we realise it or not, our relationship with our father, for good or bad, will have had far reaching consequences on our emotional wholeness as an adult and will have affected our view of the Fatherhood of God. Even those of us who were blessed with a great Dad will still have issues that bother us in adulthood, simply because there is no such thing as a perfect parent.

In a book that examines the effects of our relationship with our earthly father and how it impacts our relationship with God, it would be very easy to go down the road of behavioural psychology, but my goal here is rather to allow God to bring healing and restoration to your life through the truth of His Word. As I have seen so many times when speaking on this topic in conferences, the Holy Spirit is able to speak directly and personally to us and our situation as we trust Him and yield to His power. As you read, expect God to speak to you and be open to hear and receive what He has to say.

Throughout this book remember that the principles discussed can be broadly applied. Biblical truth and principles that apply to your relationship with your father may also apply to your relationship with your mother. Equally, they will apply if you were raised by foster parents, if you never knew your father and were raised by relatives who stepped in to help, or if you only ever knew a stepfather. God is not legalistic and He doesn't put people in boxes. Whatever your situation, be open to hearing what He has to say to you and allow Him to minister healing and wholeness to your life.

ARE YOU IN RELATIONSHIP WITH GOD?

Throughout the pages of this book one theme will stand out: relationship. We are looking at our relationship with our earthly father, our heavenly Father and His family on earth, the Body of Christ. I want you to ask yourself, "Do I have a relationship with a God who I know as my Father?" Many people know *about* God, but unless we know Him as a loving Father, then we may not truly know Him at all. If you thought of yourself as "Christian" but realise that you do not have a personal, intimate relationship with God as your Father, then you need to come to Him now through Jesus Christ, His Son.

Jesus said, *"I am the way, the truth, and the life: no man cometh unto the father, but by me"* (John 14:6). If you need to come into the reality of a relationship with God and receive assurance of your salvation, please pray the following prayer:

> "Heavenly Father, I acknowledge that I am a sinner and I need a Saviour. I repent of all my sin and invite the Lord Jesus Christ into my life that I may be born again and filled to overflowing with Your Holy Spirit. I receive You now, Lord. Thank You, Father, for the assurance of salvation and an eternity with you. Amen."

PART ONE

THE PATTERN
OF PARENTING

A Brief History of Fatherhood in Our Nation

A good place to start when trying to unravel the complexities of our relationship with our father is to try to understand the cultural/social background in which he himself was raised. Understanding where a person comes from and the factors that affected their upbringing can answer numerous questions about what makes them the person they are, why they behave like they do, why they hold certain values and beliefs, what makes them tick. I am no historian, but it is helpful to have a thumbnail sketch of recent history in order to see some of the factors which will have affected the previous generation of our fathers.

We can go back perhaps as far as World War I (1914–1918). Maybe your grandfather or great grandfather fought in that war. The death toll was such that many people went to war and never came home. The trauma resulting from that loss is still affecting lives today because so many families lost people they loved. Suddenly, fathers, brothers, uncles were snatched away and their influence taken away from the family home, never to return. The emotional tidal wave of that loss still ripples through people's lives today.

In the 1930s Britain was hit by the effects of the Depression. The Wall Street Crash of 1929 plunged the USA into economic depression and as a result they called in loans they had made to other countries and banned imported goods. The effect of this on the UK was a similar economic downturn and a sudden scarcity of jobs with 25% of the nation's workforce left unemployed. In those days there was no state benefit system like the one that exists today. Back then, if you didn't work you didn't eat. The possibility of a father (who was seen as the main bread-winner of the family, almost exclusively so then, unlike today) not being able to feed his children would have had a devastating emotional effect. There is no doubt that many men suppressed locked-up emotions as they

15

struggled with the shame of not being a provider in the family home.

Then came 1939–1945 and World War II. Along with more tragic loss of life and the trauma that brings, food was scarce and there were very few luxuries. Britain was still on rations in the early 1950s as the nation recovered from exhausting its resources to sustain the war effort. Although the war was now over and kids were growing up without the same wartime conditions, the shadow of the war still loomed large for their parents. A make-do and don't waste anything mentality persisted. Children of that era couldn't understand their parents' insistence on them eating every last morsel that was put on their dinner plate. It was true that in most homes Spam[1] featured on the menu almost every day. We thought it was normal and assumed everyone ate Spam for breakfast, dinner or tea!

Another phenomenon of the war was what later became known as "war babies". In other words, children conceived and born during the war, often with an uncertain future and with a somewhat unstable relationship between their parents. Many of these were relationships between girls and soldiers who were away from home. Years later individuals are still picking up the emotional pieces of these unions, trying to find missing fathers who were American soldiers on duty in Britain when they were born but who subsequently returned home.

By the time Britain hit the end of the 1950s and the beginning of the 1960s much had changed. It was an era when parents became obsessed with giving their children everything they had never had themselves because of the scarcity of luxuries during and immediately after the war. This is perhaps a natural reaction when one has suffered poverty and is then faced with plenty, but, needless to say, it created its own problems. Instead of bringing the happiness and satisfaction people expected, this cultural shift led people down a road of liberty and ultimately

---

1. Spam is the brand name for a pork luncheon meat.

promiscuity. This generation became the guinea pigs for the contraceptive pill and they were also the generation who learned what it meant to rebel against "the establishment". Without oversimplifying things too much, I believe this generation paved the way for the materialism, liberal attitudes and law-lessness that followed in the 1980s and 1990s.

Today, children are being born into what is rapidly devel-oping into a secular, godless society, having drifted away from the strong moral values that were so much a part of the Victorian era. The frantic pace of modern life means that many parents are, in reality, only "weekend parents" who give their children very little time and attention during the week. There are people wracked with guilt and with deep concerns that they are failing their kids and yet are on a treadmill that they can't seem to get off.

Many people today live in a fantasy world where they try to live to a standard that in reality they cannot afford. Most of our grandparents didn't know what it was to take a day off work, let alone go on an amazing holiday to a foreign country. Our ancestors worked round the clock to earn their money. They didn't have time to reflect on the psychological effects this was having on their children. All they were thinking about was how to put the next meal on the table! Many parents in this era did not know what it was to play with their children. It was a foreign concept to them. Children were left to amuse themselves. People lived from day to day and from hand to mouth. There was not a lot of joy, but people valued what they had. Today we have gone totally the other way.

So what effect has all of this had on us and therefore on our children? I believe the number one need of every child is *time*, and when life is dominated by work, or simply surviving, children are deprived of time with their parents. In the past it was because of the scarcity of resources and the long hours parents worked as a result to provide enough for their family. Today children are deprived of parental time and input because of materialism and the frantic pace of modern life. Dysfunctional adults are created when, as children, they are deprived of love, attention, encouragement and interaction. Children need to know they are safe, protected and that they are assured of the total commitment of their parents. Where that is lacking emotional trauma occurs.

God's desire is for every child to be secure and loved. He planned for that to happen naturally within the safety of normal family life, imparted through association and influence. His plan is for there to be wholeness and healing imparted through the family unit, giving every person a solid foundation for their life, yet this has been so unobtainable for so many different generations and for so many different reasons. God's purpose for every father is to play a vital role in shaping the development of his children, to encourage, love and discipline them, and to model a godly lifestyle that they can copy. This is the ideal, but it has been a reality for a minority of people.

We therefore need to allow God to bring His light into our personal situation and give us fresh revelation to put our relationship with our Dad into perspective. We need to understand more about where he came from, what circumstances shaped him into the person he is/was and how all of this affected our own development as a person.

Your Relationship with Your Dad

At the beginning of Matthew's Gospel, we read the following verses that spell out for us the lineage of Jesus Christ. It is a somewhat baffling list of names and I used to wonder as a young Christian why it was necessary to list all of this in Scripture:

> *"The book of the generation of Jesus Christ, the son of David, the son of Abraham.*
>
> *Abraham begat Isaac; and Isaac begat Jacob; and Jacob begat Judas and his brethren;*

And Judas begat Phares and Zara of Thamar; and Phares begat Esrom; and Esrom begat Aram;

And Aram begat Aminadab; and Aminadab begat Naasson; and Naasson begat Salmon;

And Salmon begat Booz of Rachab; and Booz begat Obed of Ruth; and Obed begat Jesse;

And Jesse begat David the king; and David the king begat Solomon of her that had been the wife of Urias;

And Solomon begat Roboam; and Roboam begat Abia; and Abia begat Asa;

And Asa begat Josaphat; and Josaphat begat Joram; and Joram begat Ozias;

And Ozias begat Joatham; and Joatham begat Achaz; and Achaz begat Ezekias;

And Ezekias begat Manasses; and Manasses begat Amon; and Amon begat Josias;

And Josias begat Jechonias and his brethren, about the time they were carried away to Babylon:

And after they were brought to Babylon, Jechonias begat Salathiel; and Salathiel begat Zorobabel;

And Zorobabel begat Abiud; and Abiud begat Eliakim; and Eliakim begat Azor;

And Azor begat Sadoc; and Sadoc begat Achim; and Achim begat Eliud;

And Eliud begat Eleazar; and Eleazar begat Matthan; and Matthan begat Jacob;

And Jacob begat Joseph the husband of Mary, of whom was born Jesus, who is called Christ."

(MATTHEW 1:1–16)

It seemed to me that whilst such knowledge as this might perhaps be important to people of other cultures, it wasn't particularly relevant to me. That was until God showed me one of the reasons why these verses are important: God cares where we came from. This old word "begat" simply means

19

"to bear young ... to bring forth". "Begetting" is something that is very important to God. Whoever you are and whatever the circumstances surrounding your birth, God knows about it; He knows who your father was and it matters to Him. God is aware of your lineage because it was instrumental in bringing you into this world. Where you came from was all encompassed in God's divine plan for you, to bring you into being to be a part of His family, to be loved, cherished and accepted by Him. God planned for you to exist so that you could live out the unique purpose He planned for you before the foundation of the world. Dwell on that truth for a moment. This, in itself, gives us a great deal of security: knowing that our heavenly Father knows where we have come from and has planned for us to be here! God knows and cares about our circumstances.

Together I want us to explore our relationship with our Dad. In order to do that I have listed several scenarios below. As you read through these statements highlight the ones that are relevant to you and accurately describe the kind of relationship you had/have with your father. If a statement almost, but not exactly, describes your specific situation, then feel free to adapt it to fit. Necessarily, the statements below are negative ones because we are seeking to identify, minister to and heal areas of past hurt.

- I never knew who my Dad was or anything about him
- I was adopted and I don't know much about my real father
- My mother didn't know who my father was, so I have never known
- My parents separated soon after I was born
- I knew my father, but he never lived with us
- My parents separated/divorced when I was a child
- My Dad worked all the time and was often away from home

- My Dad was always around, but still was always distant, emotionally detached
- My Dad was aggressive, violent, abusive
- My Dad was domineering, controlling and demanding
- My Dad just ignored me and never communicated with me
- My Dad became angry when I had emotional needs
- My Dad never gave me time or played with me
- My Dad let me down and I am still angry with him for it.

Having read this list (and there may be more items you want to add to it), take some time out; step back from it and reflect. Bear in mind two things as you assess what really stands out for you:

1. Remember where your Dad came from, what factors affected his upbringing and what traumas in his life made him the person he is. Have compassion for him and the circumstances that shaped him.
2. Remember that the impression you had of your Dad as a child was simply that – a childish impression. Take into account that some of the feelings you have originated as the feelings of an immature child struggling to understand. I know people who deeply resent their parents for disciplining them as children – and yet, it may have been godly discipline administered in the right way. You may need to let go of any resentment you are still harbouring now that you come to analyse it as an adult.

Many people suffer from unresolved anger they have carried over from their childhood and are still hanging onto today. The emotion of anger is produced whenever a particular goal we have is blocked. Perhaps you are angry because when you were a child you wanted money for various things and your parents wouldn't let you have it. Maybe you resent the fact that

21

your father would never let you stay out late like your friends and so you never really felt part of that circle. It's helpful to look at issues like this in the light of being an adult yourself now. Would you give your kids money for anything they wanted, especially when you can see it's just a fad? Would you be happy with your son/daughter staying out late? We have to look at issues like this through the eyes of a parent, weighing that with our parents' circumstances at the time (possibly they had less disposable income than you do now) and examine them rationally. You may not realise that you are harbouring resentment from the past unnecessarily. Have a look at the issue afresh through the eyes of an adult and you will feel differently about some of the decisions your parents made.

Other people feel bitter towards their father because they feel that he didn't love them. Maybe he seemed austere, distant to you, and you read that as a lack of interest in you. But it could be that he was behaving in the only way he knew how given his own upbringing. By applying God's grace to the situation we may be able to say that perhaps he did love us, it just didn't seem that way at the time or that's just the way we read it. Whatever particular issue is bothering you, I pray that as we continue the journey through this book you will begin to understand why your father did some of the things he did, why he didn't do things you hoped he would do, and that you find a place of freedom and release.

THE PATTERN OF PARENTING

This issue of how our father was parented and how it affected him is so important for us to grasp. Remember that just like us, our Dads were children once who had a unique experience of being parented. Your Dad's only real point of reference for being a parent is how he himself was parented. That was his starting position and it is likely that when you were born and he became a father there were far fewer resources around he could turn to for advice. These days there are dozens of books, magazines and Internet sites available with a wealth of information on parenting, but this is a recent phenomenon. A person tends to have all kinds of ideals about the kind of parent they want to be, but what they know best is what they experienced themselves.

We have a tendency to dwell on what our father did or didn't do for us, because those were the things that were important to us at the time in our childish world, but dwell for a moment on what behaviour your father learned himself as a child, what behaviour was modelled to him that he learned from and replicated. The likelihood is your Dad just muddled through, learning by trial and error, trying the techniques that he himself learned from his parents, rightly or wrongly.

Perhaps we spent a lot of time as a child expecting our father to give us things that nobody ever gave him. We should also face the reality that probably some of our childhood desires were romantic ideas and practically unreasonable. We have to be honest with ourselves and accept that some of the pain we experienced as children was self-inflicted as a result of immature selfishness.

In the following verses from Matthew 7 Jesus provided us with a brief snapshot of what a good father looks like, using the illustration to reveal to us what God is like.

"Ask, and it shall be given you; seek, and ye shall find; knock, and it shall be opened unto you: For every one that asketh receiveth; and he that seeketh findeth; and to him that knocketh it shall be opened. Or what man is there of you, whom if his son ask bread, will he give him a stone? Or if he ask a fish, will he give him a serpent? If ye then, being evil, know how to give good gifts unto your children, how much more shall your Father which is in heaven give good things to them that ask him?"

(MATTHEW 7:7–11)

Fathers are supposed to give us what we need. Some reading these verses may think, "Well, I asked often enough, but I never received." That may be true. But it may have been that our father gave us what he could, but circumstances we weren't aware of prevented him from doing more. There is also the possibility that we got the "fish" and the "serpent" confused. In other words, we asked for something that would be harmful to us, so our Dad said no and gave us something that was good for us instead. Most kids complain when they can't get what they want and often don't realise at the time that their parents are trying to help them.

Jesus illustrates for us God's ideal for a father – someone who provides for his children and nurtures them in a godly way. He says that even a father who is not a God-fearing person would basically try to do his best for his child. Sadly, we know that for many this has not been the case. Many people have known parents who neglected their needs, material and emotional. Others have experienced deception from their parents. In other words, they were told they would get a fish, but were actually handed a serpent.

It is often impossible to process our experiences until much later in life when we can look at them with a degree of perspective. As a child it is very easy to believe that what you are experiencing is "normal". Many people experienced things that at the time seemed normal, but weren't. When they looked outside of their family unit they realised that other people didn't live like that. Thankfully, God is able to heal us from the pain of those things if we bring the problem to Him.

Jesus followed His statement about fatherhood with the following instruction:

"Therefore all things whatsoever ye would that men should do to you, do ye even so to them: for this is the law and the prophets."
(MATTHEW 7:12)

The biblical ideal is that we treat all others in the way we would like to be treated ourselves. When we have yielded our lives to God and allowed Him to heal us it is easier to do so, though we can choose to do it regardless as an act of our will. But there is a saying: hurt people hurt people. People tend to treat others how they themselves have been treated. If they have experienced mistreatment in their life, a person will tend to transfer that experience onto others and treat them badly in return. Praise God that in Him we can break any cycle of hurt. Through Christ, even if we were very badly treated ourselves, we can learn a correct and godly pattern of parenting to demonstrate and pass on to our children.

2 Chronicles 26 shows such a pattern in the life of the young man Uzziah, who became king when he was just sixteen years old:

"Sixteen years old was Uzziah when he began to reign, and he reigned fifty and two years in Jerusalem ... And he did that which was right in the sight of the LORD, according to all that his father Amaziah did. And he sought God in the days of Zechariah, who had understanding in the visions of God: and as long as he sought the LORD, God made him to prosper."

(2 CHRONICLES 26:3, 4–5)

Here is a wonderful example of somebody following a good pattern provided by his father. But notice also that Uzziah needed God to be a part of the equation. He prospered as long as he sought the Lord, but he had a great head start because of the good influence on his life of the pattern laid down by his father.

Another example of a godly pattern of parenting is seen in the life of Timothy. In 2 Timothy 1:5–6 Paul, speaking to Timothy, writes,

"When I call to remembrance the unfeigned faith that is in thee, which dwelt first in thy grandmother Lois, and thy mother Eunice;

and I am persuaded that in thee also. Wherefore I put thee in
remembrance that thou stir up the gift of God, which is in thee by
the putting on of my hands."

The phrase "unfeigned faith" here means a faith that is sincere,
pure, honest and without hypocrisy. Some readers will be able
to give thanks to God that they were raised in a similar
environment to Timothy, in a godly home by God-fearing
parents. Others missed having that and need to know that
God can make it up to them and bring healing into their lives.

COMPASSION OPENS THE DOOR TO HEALING

Psalm 86:15–17 says,

"But thou, O Lord, art a God full of compassion, and gracious,
longsuffering, and plenteous in mercy and truth. O turn unto me,
and have mercy upon me; give thy strength unto thy servant, and
save the son of thine handmaid. Shew me a token for good; that they
which hate me may see it, and be ashamed: because thou, LORD,
hast holpen [helped] me, and comforted me."

Our God delights in compassion. He is longsuffering and
abundant in His desire to show mercy to us, so it pleases His
heart when we show compassion and mercy to others, even
those who have hurt us. If we are going to receive healing in
our lives from the hurt of the past and move forward in God's
purposes for our life, we need to come to a place where we
begin to show godly compassion towards our parents and
mercy for the things they got wrong with us. God can give us
that compassion if we feel unable to express it ourselves
because He delights in us copying His divine attributes. He
will help us with this if we ask Him.

"Compassion" means to have pity and the word "gracious"
in this psalm literally means to bend down towards someone,

reaching out with kindness. Like our heavenly Father we need to be "longsuffering", meaning forbearing and patient, and have an abundance of "mercy", meaning to show favour and kindness, and "truth", which in this context means trustworthiness and stability. All of these are strong words that describe the heart of God. We need to walk in these godly attributes and demonstrate them to others, but especially so to our parents.

The Bible is full of stories that reveal God's heart of compassion. I love the story about Moses being adopted by Pharaoh's daughter when he was just a few months old. His mother, in a desperate attempt to save his life, just released him into God's hands and put him into the river in a basket. His name "Moses" is apt because it means "taken out of the water". Moses was rescued and the most amazing compassion was demonstrated by God's hand upon his life. We need to see that if God can reach out and rescue a small, helpless baby and put that person on track to fulfil the destiny of their life, God's heart is the same towards each of us. If we feel abandoned, like Moses was abandoned, we need to know that God understands and has compassion towards us. Like Moses, He was there if we were abandoned by our parents or others. He saw us, He knows what happened. If He was able to pluck Moses out of the water when his fate seemed uncertain, how much more is He able to rescue us from the feelings of abandonment we have and the emotional deficit they have caused? In truth, God has been close to us all along, wanting to express His heart to us.

Throughout the Gospels we clearly see that Jesus had compassion for people. Very often it was the Lord's compassion that preceded a dramatic healing in someone's life. Compassion has to come before healing can be released. In Matthew 14:14 we read,

"And Jesus went forth, and saw a great multitude, and was moved with compassion toward them, and he healed their sick."

Jesus was often overwhelmed with compassion and it was the catalyst for Him healing many sick people. The occasion described here is particularly amazing because Jesus had only just heard the news that His cousin, John the Baptist, had been killed by beheading. What an amazing response! No doubt Satan thought this would be a bitter blow to Jesus, but it seems as if Jesus sets out to pull the rug from underneath the enemy's feet by behaving in the opposite way to that which the devil might have expected. Instead of being angry or depressed Jesus sets out to minister healing to a great multitude of people, inflicting a severe blow to the enemy's campaign to keep people in bondage.

Compassion and healing go together. The key to releasing many people's locked up emotions due to issues with their parents is to ask God for His compassion. Some reading this will have carried unresolved hurt around with them for years caused by conflict with their parents. If we can begin to have compassion for our parents, realising that they themselves have carried the hurting child of their past around with them, then we will open the door to healing in our lives. We need to uncover the issues that we have tried to bury for years and release them into God's hands because we can trust Him to heal us. We don't need to struggle on and on under those burdens. Having a godly compassion for our parents is the first step towards restoration and healing.

We can ask God to touch our spiritual eyes so that, just as Jesus touched the eyes of blind men and they received their sight back, so we will have "eyes to see". We will receive spiritual insight into our past and realise what was going on in our lives at that time; we will see the situation as it really is, as God views it. If we ask the Father may show us that if we had little leading or direction from our father it was because he received no guidance or direction from his father and he too was a victim, like us. If our father had no godly guidance in his life then really he was no better off than us. Perhaps there was never anyone there for your Dad, no one to steer him, to protect him. Without a strong father figure we are like sheep without a shepherd. There is so much in the Bible about the Lord being the One who protects us as a Shepherd. Experiencing fathering should be all about being protected. We may not have experienced that protection, but in Christ we can know the protection and shepherding of God the Father. In Christ we can receive godly guidance from the Holy Spirit and live a godly lifestyle by following the pattern of Scripture.

After compassion the next step is always forgiveness. God calls us to forgive those who have hurt us. Forgiveness is not a feeling, but an act of the will. Some of us, whose father was never there for us, may have to forgive a person we hardly knew, asking God to release His compassion in us so that we can forgive him. Whatever our circumstances were, forgiveness is essential. Jesus commands us in Matthew 18:34–35 to forgive others otherwise the mercy of God towards us will be blocked in our life. This is not a divine "suggestion" from Jesus but a commandment we have to obey. We may harbour all kinds of bitterness and unforgiveness in our hearts and try to pretend they don't exist, but eventually the Lord will catch up with us and ask us to forgive the person who wounded us, because it is for our own wellbeing. If this is a new concept for some, then we need to realise that here lies the road to freedom. The Holy Spirit can give us divine insight into our specific situation so that we know how we should pray about it. With the Father's help we can address the issues of our past, apply compassion and show forgiveness.

THE CURSE OF DISOBEDIENCE

Psalm 109 has some sobering words about what happens to the children of "wicked" men. In other words, men who don't know the Lord and don't walk in His ways. There are consequences for the children of those who reject God.

"Wicked" may sound like a harsh word to use, you may think, "My Dad didn't know Jesus, but he wasn't 'wicked'." But the Bible teaches that where there is no godly pattern of life imparted to the next generation then there is sin, and sin is wickedness in God's eyes and has to be judged.

> *"Hold not thy peace, O God of my praise; for the mouth of the wicked and the mouth of the deceitful are opened against me: they have spoken against me with a lying tongue. They compassed me about also with words of hatred; and fought against me without a cause. For my love they are my adversaries: but I give myself unto prayer. And they have rewarded me evil for good, and hatred for my love. Set thou a wicked man over him: and let Satan stand at his right hand. When he shall be judged, let him be condemned: and let his prayer become sin. Let his days be few; and let another take his office."*

> (PSALM 109:1–8)

These verses speak about various aspects of the lives of the ungodly who are pursuing a sinful lifestyle. Then, beginning in verse 9, we read of the consequences that result from that lifestyle and how it affects that next generation:

> *"Let his children be fatherless, and his wife a widow.*
> *Let his children be continually vagabonds, and beg: let them seek their bread also out of their desolate places.*
> *Let the extortioner catch all that he hath; and let the strangers spoil his labour.*
> *Let there be none to extend mercy unto him: neither let there be any to favour his fatherless children. Let his posterity be cut off; and in the generation following let their name be blotted out.*
> *Let the iniquity of his fathers be remembered with the LORD; and let not the sin of his mother be blotted out.*
> *Let them be before the LORD continually, that he may cut off the memory of them from the earth. Because that he remembered not to*

shew mercy, but persecuted the poor and needy man, that he might even slay the broken in heart.

As he loved cursing, so let it come unto him: as he delighted not in blessing, so let it be far from him. As he clothed himself with cursing like as with his garment, so let it come into his bowels like water, and like oil into his bones.

Let it be unto him as the garment which covereth him, and for a girdle wherewith he is girded continually.

Let this be the reward of mine adversaries from the LORD, and of them that speak evil against my soul."

(PSALM 109:9–20)

And so it continues. We can see that there is a very definite curse that comes upon the children of people who act wickedly before God. The curse is the self-inflicted result of disobedience to Him and His ways. Those who ignore God or set themselves against Him and His ways may suffer barrenness, widowhood/divorce as a result. The Bible says that their children are like "vagabonds", and this is an appropriate term because it describes someone who roams, can't settle anywhere and is directionless. Poverty is another aspect of this curse. It does not necessarily mean a person will be destitute, but that they could work and work and yet their career could be fruitless and they may feel as though they are getting nowhere.

Most of us would probably think of our father, if they didn't know the Lord, as being well-meaning but essentially misguided. That may be the case, but the effects of ignoring God and His ways will be the same. Thankfully, as believers we can break the power of any curse that tries to limit us as a result of the sin of our ancestors, because Jesus dealt with every curse at the cross:

"Christ hath redeemed us from the curse of the law, being made a curse for us: for it is written, Cursed is every one that hangeth on a tree."

(GALATIANS 3:13)

31

Whatever pattern of parenting our father demonstrated to us, praise God that we are now in a position as His children to come under His perfect parenting. We know too that He is able to heal the hurts of the past. Reflect on the following points and pray through the prayers at the end of this section.

SUMMARY

- We need to accept that although we can ask questions and investigate to an extent, we will probably never fully understand the factors that made our father who he is: what events and influences shaped his life and were therefore instrumental in influencing how he related to us. What we do know is that no person ever had a perfect upbringing and many things could have caused our father to be less than the ideal, biblical model we might have hoped for. Therefore we need to ask God to help us show compassion for our father and forgive him for the things he did that may have left us hurt or confused. Compassion and forgiveness are the keys that will open the door to your healing.

- You may not have had a godly pattern to follow in your formative years, possibly even if you grew up in a Christian home. Choose to forgive your father for either not modelling a godly lifestyle or for not imparting it to you.

- No one experiences lasting change in their life without being hungry for it. God the Father is full of compassion and if we really want to be healed we just need to cry out to Him and say, "Lord, I want some of Your compassion, I want You to teach me, I want to be able to forgive so that I'm set free."

- Some reading this may need to acknowledge for the first time how deeply they have been affected by their relationship with their father and come to the place where they are prepared to lay that down before God. This will mean saying that we don't want to put 100% of the blame on our Dad. There may have been accusations and hard hearts in the past, but you can release all of that to the Lord now.

- We can give thanks for the fact that, though our parents may not have known God or guided us into a godly pattern of life, just like Moses we have been "rescued from the water". God has found us and saved us in our helplessness and He can restore to us all that we have "lost" through absent parents or dysfunctional relationships.

— *Prayers* —

Below are various prayers to help you to pray into your specific situation.

A prayer to release forgiveness to your father:

"Heavenly Father, You know my heart. I bring my life before You. I bring my father/guardian before You and as an act of my will I choose to forgive any circumstance, known or unknown, that has touched my life. I choose this road of obedience before You and I receive my freedom in Jesus' name. By Your power release me from any torment in my mind, body and soul. Divinely impart to me supernatural compassion and spiritual insight to see my past through Your eyes and bring Your healing to me, in Jesus' name. Amen. Thank You, Father God."

Those who feel it is appropriate for them can pray about curses brought about by the sins of their forefathers. We don't always understand the depth of such generational ties, but we can be totally free from their influence by the power of Jesus. We can pray for God to release us from any curse of barrenness and poverty, widowhood/divorce. We can also pray to be set free from the curse of the vagabond where people never feel they have a secure resting place or feel at peace.

> "Father, I thank You for the power of the blood of Jesus that cancels out and breaks the power of every curse. I pray now, God, that You would release me from any curse resulting from the ungodly, sinful ways of my ancestors and I pray that You would fill my heart with Your peace in the name of Jesus. Thank You, Father, that Your peace will replace those feelings of restlessness and of not belonging. Thank You that I have peace and security in You and that I belong to Your family. Amen."

> "Father God, I pray that you would break the curse of poverty over my life – emotionally, mentally, physically, financially – and I pray that You would release Your favour over my life. Father, thank You that wherever there has been barrenness, poverty and destruction in my life You can restore it and bring me to wholeness through Jesus Christ. Father, I thank You for the prosperity and abundance You are releasing into my life and I receive it now in Jesus' name. Amen."

The psalmist wrote, *"My spirit is overwhelmed within me, my heart is desolate."* Often people feel a sense of desolation that lurks in the background of their life and never leaves them and they don't know why. That feeling of desolation can be caused by abandonment that occurs at one level or another in our lives.

It may be that you feel you were betrayed by your father at some point, or that you were unwanted, maybe even from the womb.

"Father, You know my heart. You know all about the feelings of desolation, abandonment and rejection I have felt. I release my hurt to You now and I choose to forgive my parents before You now for their part in it. Please break the stronghold of desolation in my life and where there has been a lack of hope, fill my life with Your hope, peace and love. Minister Your healing into my life. Break the mental images that I have in my soul to do with painful memories, divinely erase them and write over them with Your truth and love. Break the power of self-pity in my life and don't let me hold on to anything that will harm me. Thank You, Holy Spirit, for ministering freedom in my life, in Jesus' name. Amen."

The effect of not being wanted as a child is a deep-seated trauma that lasts into adulthood. Whether you were, in your parents' eyes, an "accident" or they hoped you would be the opposite sex, it is destructive and debilitating to your emotional wholeness. Some people have lived with the suspicion of their parents' feelings though nothing has ever been said, whilst others have had it said to their faces. Either way it has a profound effect and prevents people from moving forward into the fullness of their lives. God can set us free from this because there are no mistakes, no accidents, no unwanted children and no illegitimate children in His family.

"Father, I thank You that I am chosen and dearly loved by You (Colossians 3:12). Thank You that You planned and purposed for me from the foundation of the earth and that I belong in Your family. I pray that You will break the power of any curse spoken over me knowingly or unknowingly in the womb; that You would break the power of all the negative things that have been spoken over me. I pray, Father, that You would release me to be the person You created me to be, free from the limitations spoken over me by others. I choose to forgive my parents for their attitudes towards me. Thank You, Father, for imparting life to me and for making me whole by the power of Your Holy Spirit, in Jesus' name. Amen."

— *Further scriptures for reflection* —

There are those who have absolutely no knowledge whatso-ever of their genetic father and this creates a strong sense of isolation and abandonment. But the truth is, if this applies to you, God the Father knows you and wants you to live in the truth that you are planned and wanted by Him. Remember earlier in this chapter we looked at genealogies in the Bible and thought about how much it matters to God where people come from. God ordained that you should be born. Wherever we came from and whatever the circumstances were that surrounded our birth, we are chosen and loved by God. Your Father knows you even if you never knew your father. Take time to reflect on the following scripture:

"If I take the wings of the morning, and dwell in the uttermost parts of the sea; even there shall thy hand lead me, and thy right hand shall hold me. If I say, Surely the darkness shall cover me; even the night shall be light about me. Yea, the darkness hideth not from thee; but the night shineth as the day: the darkness and the light are both alike to thee. For thou hast possessed my reins: thou hast covered me in my mother's womb. I will praise thee; for I am fearfully and wonderfully made: marvellous are thy works; and that my soul knoweth right well. My substance was not hid from thee, when I was made in secret, and curiously wrought in the lowest

parts of the earth. Thine eyes did see my substance, yet being unperfect; and in thy book all my members were written, which in continuance were fashioned, when as yet there was none of them. How precious also are thy thoughts unto me, O God! How great is the sum of them! If I should count them, they are more in number than the sand: when I awake, I am still with thee."

(PSALM 139:9–18)

Wow! Father God made me in secret and saw my unformed frame and all the days of my life were written before they happened!

Each one of us can know the reality of being adopted into the family of God and be totally secure in our identity as one of His children through Christ. God knows us intimately; He knows every hair on our heads.

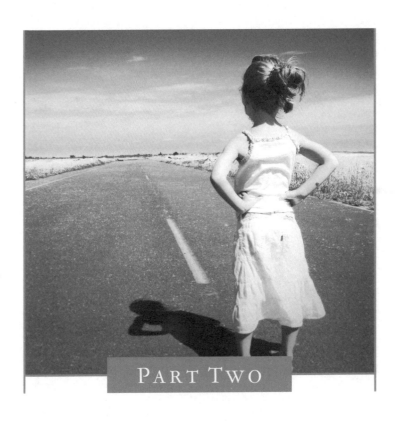

PART TWO

WHAT OUR FATHERS SHOULD HAVE DONE FOR US...

WHAT OUR FATHERS SHOULD HAVE DONE FOR US ACCORDING TO GOD'S WORD

In the previous section we looked at the fact that we need to have a revelation about the factors that affected our father and influenced how he parented us. We saw the need for compassion and forgiveness to open up the path to our healing. In this section we will look at a biblical pattern of what our father should have done for us according to God's Word, firstly so that we can understand something of what we have perhaps missed out on, and secondly so that we can grasp the principles of godly parenting and apply them ourselves.

THE PATTERN OF DEUTERONOMY 6

Rather than thinking about all the things we wished our fathers had done for us and didn't, we need to look at this issue from God's perspective. If God has ordained a pattern of living for us and spelled it out in His Word then we need to look at that and follow it. This will mean letting go of some of those things that have been issues for us personally, that perhaps we have held onto childishly, and learning to cooperate with God's plan. We have to accept that God knows what is required in order to make us a whole, complete people who have a firm foundation for their lives, and we need to trust Him to do that, restoring and repairing our foundations as necessary.

In studying examples of fathering in the Bible it is amazing how many references there are to being given direction and discipline, and how these verses far outweigh other scriptures on the subject of fathering. For many, that's probably the last thing we want to hear! After all, no child naturally enjoys being told what to do or being disciplined. But the Bible insists that this is central to the role of a good father.

Deuteronomy chapter 6 lays down a foundation for biblical parenting because here God tells His people both how they should live and how to impart it to their children.

> *"Now these are the commandments, the statutes, and the judgments, which the LORD your God commanded to teach you, that ye might do them in the land whither ye go to possess it: that thou mightest fear the LORD thy God, to keep all his statutes and his commandments, which I command thee, thou, and thy son, and thy son's son, all the days of thy life; and that thy days may be prolonged."*
>
> (DEUTERONOMY 6:1–2)

We see that there is a conditional promise for people who obey God's commandments and share these truths with their children and grandchildren:

> *"Hear therefore, O Israel, and observe to do it; that it may be well with thee* [another promise]*, and that ye may increase mightily, as the LORD God of thy fathers hath promised thee, in the land that floweth with milk and honey. Hear, O Israel: The LORD our God is one LORD: And thou shalt love the LORD thy God with all thine heart, and with all thy soul, and with all thy might. And these words, which I command thee this day, shall be in thine heart."*
>
> (VERSES 3–6)

Then comes the specific commission to the fathers in verses 7–8 which tells us that in every aspect of life, children should be receiving direction from their father:

> *"And thou shalt teach them diligently unto thy children, and shalt talk of them when thou sittest in thine house, and when thou walkest by the way, and when thou liest down, and when thou risest up. And thou shalt bind them for a sign upon thine hand, and they shall be as frontlets between thine eyes."*
>
> (VERSES 7–8)

1. Our father should have taught and trained us through everyday life

In biblical times these commands of God were so important to His people that they took His instructions to bind them on their hands and foreheads literally. The commands were written on tiny strips of parchment and enclosed in small leather boxes called phylacteries which were then bound to their upper arms and foreheads, to be worn during weekday prayers. Since Jesus imparted the Holy Spirit to us these commands are written on our hearts rather than worn physically. But what is very clear in these verses is the pattern for guiding our children. We see the constant godly influence of the parent at work, with the child receiving instruction whether they are relaxing at home or out of the house doing other things. Notice that the verse also covers the beginning and the end of the day. In other words, godly instruction should be happening twenty-four-seven.

God's view is that every aspect of the day should be a time of tuition and education for a child. The lives of godly parents should provide a pattern so that there is a constant, open witness of how to live. God's method of applying truth is profound, because don't we all know that it's no good someone telling us something unless they live by what they say? People have to lead by example and demonstrate the truth, otherwise what they say they stand for counts for very little. And a demonstration of the truth is so much more powerful if it is a natural, everyday thing.

To instil values into a child a parent has to both model them and communicate them. A key time to do this is at meal times when the family all gather together around the table to talk and share food together. It saddens me that this important godly lifestyle seems to have been lost to a great extent from family life in the West. It was and still is vitally important in Jewish culture, which lies at the roots of our faith, and this is the reason why: to impart godly values in a natural environment.

Family leisure time is equally important and this too seems to be lacking in so many families. Just spending time together at leisure, having fun, can be so instructive for children and helps build a firm foundation in their lives.

Verse 7 also emphasizes children's bedtime and early morning routines. How children are put to bed at night and what happens when they wake up the next morning is so important when training them. Bedtime can be a special time to spend with your children. At the end of the day when they are tired they often need that assurance of protection for the night. What better way to give it than to pray for our kids as they go off to sleep and then start the next day by praying and committing the day to God? It shows a total involvement from the father and creates an atmosphere of protection in the home.

Of course, if our fathers didn't know God or His Word then they could not have lived it or applied it, in which case we have missed out. Maybe our father was a Christian but failed to teach us godly principles. Whatever your circumstances were, bring them before the Father and allow your heart to forgive your Dad for not raising you according to God's Word. Some fathers will have never heard the Word of God, others will have heard it and rejected it. We can choose to forgive them and ask the Lord to make up for that lost time in our lives.

2. ... Prayed for us
The Bible makes it clear that fathers should pray for their children. One example is Lamentations 2:19:

> *"Arise, cry out in the night: in the beginning of the watches pour out thine heart like water before the face of the LORD: lift up thy hands toward him for the life of thy young children..."*

Prayer is valuable input into a person's life. Maybe our father prayed for us, maybe he didn't. The Bible paints a vivid picture of a father lifting up his hands to God on behalf of his children, but again, if our father didn't pray for us and commit us to the Lord, we need to forgive him and accept the incredible truth that Jesus Himself is interceding for us. Even if we never knew our father, Jesus is our mediator and He is standing in the gap for us.

"For there is one God, and one mediator between God and men, the man Christ Jesus."

(1 TIMOTHY 2:5)

3. . . . Shown us the way of salvation

Fathers should be instrumental in showing their children the way of salvation. Paul writing to Timothy says,

"And that from a child thou hast known the holy scriptures, which are able to make thee wise unto salvation through faith which is in Christ Jesus. All scripture is given by inspiration of God, and is profitable for doctrine, for reproof, for correction, for instruction in righteousness: that the man of God may be perfect, throughly furnished unto all good works."

(2 TIMOTHY 3:15–17)

Timothy, although no mention is made of his father, did have the godly influence of his mother and grandmother and as a result was knowledgeable in the Word of God from a young age. What a great foundation for his life.

4. . . . Applied godly discipline

There are many scriptures relating to discipline. Proverbs 29:15 says,

"The rod and reproof give wisdom: but a child left to himself bringeth his mother to shame."

There is a great deal of contention in society today regarding discipline with many movements wanting to ban smacking and even have parents arrested for assault for disciplining their children in this way. I believe this is a not too subtle attempt to undermine the godly values and principles of the Bible. According to God the "rod" should be used to bring discipline in order to train a child. The problem occurs, of course, when discipline is meted out without love and a godly commitment to the child's wellbeing, because then it is seen as and can be "abuse". Too often, however, our nation seems to side with the vocal minority who want to take away this right from parents, without seeing the bigger picture or wanting to know what God's direction is. As you read this you may think, "I don't believe in smacking", but God tells us to use a rod as part of godly parenting.

It's interesting that God says to use a "rod". Perhaps this is because the hands should only be used for blessing? In other words, an implement is used for correction because the hand of blessing should not be used to strike a person. We don't know the reason because the Bible doesn't tell us, so have to accept that God knows best. The Hebrew word for "reproof" has a broad meaning and doesn't just mean telling the child off. It includes chastisement but also correction, rebuke and reasoning. This means that discipline is not a one-off event that happens when a child is naughty, but a continuous, ongoing event where there exists a rapport between parent and child and things are talked over and reasoned through. Rather than there simply being a rebuke and the rod, there is a conversation and an explanation of why behaviour needs to change. This is the godly pattern. The rod is used only when the child refuses to listen to reason.

Another interesting aspect here is that a lack of discipline affects a child's relationship with their mother. The word "shame" in Hebrew means to be ashamed or disappointed. It is a terrible thing for a mother to feel disappointed in her children. The word also means to be "confused" or "confounded", implying a sense of not knowing what is going on or how to rectify it.

Very few people will ever say that when they were a child they were in agreement with their father correcting them. Most of us were running away from discipline not embracing it. But the ideal is that discipline is meted out in a godly way, with love, because it is for the child's benefit. It may be that some readers will need to forgive their father if discipline for them was handled badly. Perhaps your father only ever disciplined you out of anger or frustration. Maybe the opposite was true – that your father was too soft and never disciplined you at all, let alone disciplining you too much, and this led you to believe that he wasn't interested in you and didn't really care about you. This has certainly been the case for some people.

But regardless of our specific circumstances, the Bible insists that discipline is necessary, and that it is a sign of love. The father who loves his child brings correction (see Proverbs 13:24). People who had fathers who only gave them what they wanted rather than what they needed often find it hard when they go out into the world and begin relating to other people. If they have been used to getting their own way and lacked discipline and correction, then they will have a rude awakening because other people will not respond to them like their father did and they will probably have a tough time.

Proverbs 22:15 says,

"Foolishness is bound in the heart of a child; but the rod of correction shall drive it far from him."

It is a revelation we all need to grasp that God says where there is foolishness in our hearts as children, godly discipline will deal with it and drive it out of us. So many of us have gone on living with some degree of foolishness in our hearts and we are still trying to sort ourselves out! If we don't want to be foolish, then we need to submit to God's discipline.

5. ... *Taught us how to manage money (Proverbs 22:6)*

This might seem a surprising aspect of discipline and correction that God brings into the mix, but how vital it is! It is so important that a father gives his children guidance on how to live practically, how to handle their finances and how to live sensibly. Look at the parable of the prodigal son that Jesus told. In the story the father had to make a decision whether to prevent his son from going off or whether to release him along with his inheritance. Rightly or wrongly the father in the story released his son and the son immediately squandered all his money until he was destitute.

If our father didn't give us any direction regarding the stewardship of our money or goods then we have missed out and we may be able to identify this as being the root of certain struggles that we have handling money as an adult. We may be missing out firstly because our father had no concept of giving to God and such concepts as tithing or giving were alien to him, in which case we are forfeiting the blessings that result from giving to God. But we may also find ourselves living under a yoke of poverty where all the money we earn seems to vanish in a second and we constantly feel we are struggling to keep our head above water. Perhaps we were given godly financial patterns but departed from them. Repentance is needed again!

We must choose to forgive our fathers for their ignorance or lack of obedience in this area and ask God to give us the revelation of biblical financial management that is so clearly laid out in the Scriptures. However badly we were trained in the past we have a responsibility to put right the issues that the Holy Spirit highlights and to begin to walk in the light of God's Word. It may be that growing up we saw our parents frittering money away and getting into debt and we thought that was "normal" because it was modelled for us and imparted to us on a daily basis. But we know that according to Scripture that is not a godly way to live. So we need the Lord to come and help us make radical changes. Where there has been a pattern of money not being used wisely we need the Lord to bring deliverance and healing to our souls and revelation for us to put it right.

THE BIBLICAL PARENT–CHILD RELATIONSHIP

The Bible presents a clear picture of how the relationship between a child and his/her parents is meant to function and it expresses what the child's attitude should be and also the parents' attitude. In his letter to the Ephesians the apostle Paul writes,

> *"Children, obey your parents in the Lord: for this is right. Honour thy father and mother; which is the first commandment with promise; that it may be well with thee, and thou mayest live long on the earth. And, ye fathers, provoke not your children to wrath: but bring them up in the nurture and admonition of the Lord."*
>
> (EPHESIANS 6:1–4)

1. Obedience and respect

The most important thing for children is to show obedience and respect towards their parents. Ideally, respect should flow both ways! The issue of respect is a massive one in our nation right now and people are beginning to wake up to the fact that where it is not instilled into young people's lives it will lead to all kinds of devastating results. In our own hearts we may need to repent of the fact that we didn't obey or show respect to our parents when we were younger, whether through ignorance or sheer rebellion. Whatever the reason, we need to repent and ask God to forgive us for our disobedience.

We also need to ask the Lord to forgive us and set us free if we have never "honoured" our father and mother as His Word commands. Honouring our parents does not mean we have to agree with everything they say and do. It doesn't mean bowing the knee to them and going along with everything they say if it doesn't line up with the Word of God – because God's Word overrules any ungodly direction our parents give us. It simply means honouring them for their *position* as our parents, as the people who were instrumental in bringing us into this world. God wants us to honour our parents or guardians, whoever filled that role for us and sought to raise as best they knew how, as an act of our will. We choose to honour them because God commands it and with His help we can begin to see the world through their eyes and apply compassion.

If we choose to honour our parents in obedience to God then He can actually begin to bring healing to us for all that has happened in the past. If we hang on to hurt, misunderstanding and bitterness then we will never be free. Honouring our parents not only sets us free from the baggage of the past, but it releases the blessing that God promised that it will be well with us and we will live a long life and be prosperous.

2. Nurturing not provoking

Ephesians 6:4 is a key verse for fathers where we read,

> *"And, ye fathers, provoke not your children to wrath: but bring them up in the nurture and admonition of the Lord."*

"Provoke" and "wrath" are the same word in the Greek and mean to enrage, provoke or anger. The word "nurture" here means tutorage and implies disciplinary correction, education, training, instruction and chastening.

What would provoke a child and make them angry? Usually it is the unfairness and feelings of injustice that are caused by correction being applied in an ungodly way. Also by bullying and by the sometimes violent discipline that is brought instantly without discussion and the dimension of reasoning mentioned earlier. Also disciplinary measures that are unrealistic and ill thought through will provoke a child. Another form of provocation is a lack of clear disciplinary boundaries so that the child knows what is acceptable behaviour and what is not. Blurred boundaries will always cause frustration and result in bad behaviour from a child.

Provocation can also be caused by constant nit picking and nagging. Correction is necessary, but when it is out of balance and children are constantly "picked on" for trivial things this creates a barrier between child and parent. It can turn children into nervous wrecks and it can also confuse them because often trivial matters become the focus of the parents' attention while bigger matters are ignored. Children get frustrated and upset whenever they see inconsistency in their parents' behaviour.

This scripture tells us we need to guide our children, train them and, when necessary, admonish them. The word "admonish" here means to call to attention, to give a mild rebuke or warning. Again the Bible is painting the picture of parenting as it should be: a continuous and ongoing relationship where the parent is continually imparting advice and wisdom to the child, correcting them and warning them about things where necessary. This is the key to nurturing a child and not frustrating them so that they rebel.

3. Discouragement

Paul repeats his advice about provocation in his letter to the Colossians and adds a further reason:

> "Fathers, provoke not your children to anger, **lest they be discouraged.**"
>
> (COLOSSIANS 3:21, emphasis added)

If you continually provoke your children to anger they will grow up discouraged and it will badly affect their lives. Discouragement is a powerful tool in the hands of the enemy and it can exert tremendous power over a person's life. Discouragement can change the direction of a person's life, affect how they handle relationships with other people, affect

51

how they behave in the workplace and cause a whole host of other problems. Discouragement is like a cloud constantly hanging over a person's life. The Greek word Paul used here that we translate "discouraged" means to be spiritless and disheartened. Discouragement crushes a person's spirit and heart and causes them to lose their identity. It is a finely balanced thing to bring correction to a child but still allow them to keep their personality and unique character traits, to correct them but to not bring discouragement. We need to make a habit of encouraging our children and praising/ rewarding them for good behaviour, whilst keeping in mind to apply continual, gentle correction and guidance.

4. Physical touch

Discipline is more easily accepted by children where there is a foundation of appropriate physical touch and intimacy. Whilst we know that there can be inappropriate physical contact and abuse, we also know that a father showing physical affection towards his children is vitally important. Wherever children have missed out on this it always affects their relationships and the way in which they interact with others later in life.

The Bible paints a picture of the importance of physical contact. Genesis 31:55 says,

"And early in the morning Laban rose up, and kissed his sons and his daughters, and blessed them…"

We also see that when the prodigal son returned home it was his father who saw him, ran to him, hugged him and kissed him, showing him a heart of compassion. Contact between fathers and daughters and fathers and sons is so vital to a child's wholeness. Some people are naturally more tactile than others and some people need to touch and be touched more than others, but know that if you feel you missed out on this, God can fill that gap in your life.

SUMMARY

- God has ordained a biblical pattern for raising children so that they develop into whole, well-balanced people. A vital part of this pattern is the application of godly discipline. But although godly discipline is necessary in a child's life, discipline administered wrongly or with wrong motivations can be very damaging. Discipline can be misused and abused when parents mete it out in the heat of the moment in anger or with violence. We need to forgive our parents if they treated us badly when trying to discipline or correct us in their own flawed way. Where discipline was always given in anger we need to ask for God's healing touch on our lives. If we truly want to walk in freedom then we have to trust the Father enough to bring this issue before Him, putting aside our fear and denial, and facing it head on. Remember that our fathers copied whatever pattern they themselves were raised with, but in Christ we can break every ungodly pattern of behaviour and move on.

- We also need to forgive our parents where there was a complete lack of discipline which left us feeling ignored and uncared for. Perhaps our parents lacked any kind of parenting skills or were just indifferent to our needs and therefore didn't take the time to discipline us. But thank God that He is able to restore to us what we missed out on.

- Discouragement brought about by ungodly discipline can be very debilitating. Where a person's spirit has been broken by constant discouragement healing needs to be released. God is able to restore our souls and revive our wounded spirits.

— *Prayers* —

A prayer to release forgiveness and receive healing for harsh discipline:

"Father, You know my situation better than anyone and know how I was raised. You know that at times I was disciplined in anger and felt the shame and humiliation of that. I pray that You would break the power of violence that was used against me and break any pattern of aggression in my life. Forgive me for all the times that I have been provoked to anger myself because of discipline that was unreasonable and ungodly. I pray that You would release Your compassion through me, the love and compassion of Jesus, to my parents. I choose now to forgive them that I might be healed and made whole by You, Lord. I choose to forgive so that there will be no spiritual blockages in my life and I will be free to walk with You in Your power. Thank You, Jesus. Amen."

A prayer for those whose father never disciplined them:

"Father God, You know that because my Dad never corrected or guided me that I have felt a lack of love. I pray that You would set me free from any 'foolishness' that still remains in my character due to that lack of discipline. I forgive my parents for not guiding or correcting me, for not bringing godly discipline into my life when I needed it and I pray You would bring healing and restoration to my heart and help me to yield to Your fatherly discipline and correction which is a sign of Your love for me. I pray You would bring healing to my heart for the confusion I have felt in the past and help from now on to live according to a godly pattern as Your Word commands. Amen."

A prayer to receive wisdom concerning good stewardship:

"Father, I was never given godly instruction concerning finance or generally taught how to be wise with money. I forgive my parents in Jesus' name. My finances are a mess and I know I am not walking in the fullness of Your abundance. I pray You will open my eyes to the Scriptures on godly giving and that I would be a cheerful giver. I know You can turn my finances around as I apply obedience. I ask You to break this yoke of poverty on me in Jesus' name. I thank You now for a bountiful harvest in my life. Amen."

A prayer for those who have suffered with discouragement:

"Father God, I thank You that You are for me and always want the best for me and that Your heart is to encourage me and help me to reach my potential in Christ. I bring before You all the discouragement and hurt that I have suffered in the past and I release it to You now in Jesus' name. I choose to forgive my parents for the things they said and did which helped to form that discouragement in me and I release them from any blame. I choose the path of showing compassion to them for all the discouragement they must have received themselves. I ask for Your healing touch on my life and I thank You that by Your power You can reverse the effects of that discouragement and bring me to a place of fresh hope. In Jesus' name. Amen."

Discouragement tends to shut people down emotionally and causes their personalities to be stunted and inhibited. It can make a person feel worthless and rejected but Jesus can cleanse and restore us by the power of His blood.

"Father God, You understand that I have often suffered with feelings of worthlessness and rejection. I confess before You now that those feelings are a lie from the Enemy and I take authority over them now in the name of Jesus. Discouragement in the past has robbed me of hope, but I pray that You will restore Your hope to me now in Jesus' name. I pray that You would minister healing to my wounded soul. Release me into the liberty that Jesus has won for me. Thank You that the truth is that I am accepted by the Father. I choose to walk in my inheritance in Christ and in my authority as a child of God. Thank You, Father. Amen."

A prayer for those who missed out on physical affection as a child:

"Father God, I pray that You would minister healing to my soul and fill the gap that should have been filled by affection from my Dad and Mum. Heal me and make me whole so that I won't try to manipulate and control others to give me the affection I've missed. I reach out to You and embrace You. Help me to reach out and show affection, and not withhold my physical touch from those I love. I thank You that You are able to restore to me all the years the locusts have eaten. Thank You, Father, in Jesus' name. Amen."

PART THREE

RECONCILIATION

RECONCILIATION FOR PRODIGALS

"And he arose, and came to his father. But when he was yet a great way off, his father saw him, and had compassion, and ran, and fell on his neck, and kissed him. And the son said unto him, Father, I have sinned against heaven, and in thy sight, and am no more worthy to be called thy son. But the father said to his servants, Bring forth the best robe, and put it on him; and put a ring on his hand, and shoes on his feet: And bring hither the fatted calf, and kill it; and let us eat, and be merry: For this my son was dead, and is alive again; he was lost, and is found. And they began to be merry."

(LUKE 15:20–24)

The story of the prodigal son is a powerful and amazing one because it speaks of reconciliation. We see in it a son who goes off the rails and begins to follow a path in life that would ultimately lead to his ruin and destruction – were he to pursue it to the bitter end. But that son is restored to his father. Not only does his father accept him back without making mention of all the foolish things he has done, but he restores him to a place of honour and throws a huge celebration. The father just rejoices in the fact that here is his son who has seen the folly of his ways and returned home. He has a son again!

Most of us can think of times in our lives where we have gone off and done something foolish. For most, however, it's unlikely that we received the same degree of unconditional love that the father in the story showed to his errant son. When we did things wrong was there true reconciliation with our parents? Was there love and understanding and forgiveness? Were we given godly direction? Was our father a mediator in the home who helped us to solve problems in our relationships with our siblings? Was there a time in your life when you were pretty foolish but your father didn't handle it very well and it just brought more hurt?

God's ideal is for us to be accepted back after we have made foolish mistakes, once we recognise it and are repentant. But not all of us had such a relationship with our earthly dads. For many there were times when we messed up and really needed to be loved and forgiven by our father, readily, unconditionally, and for him to say, "It's OK. Let's look at this together so it doesn't happen again." It is a natural response that when we act foolishly and we apologise for our actions, we want the person we have aggrieved to show that they trust us again. We want to know that we haven't blotted our copybook forever as far as they are concerned. But if this was not the case for you with your Dad, you need to know that you can receive God's healing power right now to set you free from the guilt and shame of the past. Where your soul has been wounded by your father's rejection, Jesus can revive it and bring it to life again. Reconciliation and forgiveness with your earthly dad may or may not be possible, but Jesus can heal and restore you just the same. Look at the prayer at the end of this section to work through this issue with God.

We see again here the truth that we need God's compassion to be at work in us when dealing with our relationship with our father. Maybe he was not able to show compassion for us and release forgiveness to us when we most needed it, but remember that he was conditioned by his own upbringing and unique set of circumstances to respond to you in the way that he did. Whether we know exactly what those circumstances were or not, having compassion for him is the first step towards healing. We will walk free when we ask God to help us decide to release that compassion towards our father and any others who have hurt us in the past.

The parable tells us that the son was received back unconditionally when he presented himself to his father with a repentant heart. He went with humility. In fact, the story tells us, in his mind he thought he might be able to work as one of his father's servants and live somewhere on his estate. His view was that he had messed up so much that he had no idea he would be accepted back as a son, let alone a fully fledged son with all his rights restored and be received back into the family home. The realisation of his unworthiness to receive such a blessing must have made an incredible impact on him as he returned home. Just like this young man, we need to have a similar humility and a repentant heart to be able to receive all the healing Father God wants to give us. In laying everything in our life down before Him we can experience the security of being accepted as sons and daughters of God.

The prodigal son received a robe, a ring and shoes to show that he had been restored. These gifts set him apart from the hired hands in his father's household and signified his position of sonship. Similarly God gives us a robe of righteousness to signify our position of acceptedness in His household and to show that we have all the rights of a son in His kingdom. God throws a celebration in heaven as we accept our position as a son or daughter in His house.

PRODIGALS WHO REJECTED THE GODLY WAYS OF THEIR PARENTS

In 1 Samuel 8:3 we read about what happened to the sons of the great prophet Samuel. Samuel came to prominence as a servant of God at a time when there was a barrenness of the Word of God in the land. He became God's mouthpiece and was used powerfully by Him. He played a critical role in anointing David, whom God had chosen to succeed Saul, as the future king of Israel. It seems amazing then that Samuel's sons did not follow the Lord in the same way and became rebellious, but the Bible says,

"And his sons walked not in his ways, but turned aside after lucre [money], and took bribes, and perverted judgment ... And [the

elders of Israel] said unto him, Behold, thou art old, and thy sons walk not in thy ways..."

(1 SAMUEL 8:3, 5)

Samuel had made his sons judges over Israel, but they became corrupt. Sometimes, despite having the best role model who endeavoured to teach them and guide them in godly ways, people simply reject it and take a different path. If we have done that ourselves then we need to bring that before the Lord and repent of it. It is a serious matter to have rejected the godly ways of our parents, that although we were given the best start in life we could have asked for, we rejected it and chose another way. But thank God, He is merciful and gracious and accepts back all those who are repentant as Jesus' parable of the prodigal illustrates.

NEGATIVE PARENTAL INFLUENCES

Some people will find themselves in the opposite position – instead of rebelling against the godly guidance of their parents they found themselves coming under the influence of their parents' ungodly behaviour and this had a very negative effect on them. There are numerous examples in Scripture, but the example of Herodias and her daughter, described in Matthew's Gospel chapter 14, particularly stands out.

King Herod was having an adulterous relationship with Herodias, the wife of his brother Philip. Matthew intimates that John knew about this and had already rebuked Herod for it, telling him he was acting unlawfully. As a result Herod had seized John and put him in prison (Matthew 14:3–4). He stopped short of simply putting John to death, however, because he was afraid of the people who revered John as a prophet. And this, as the text implies, was despite pressure from Herodias to do so. But Herodias was out for revenge and would stop at nothing, even using her own daughter to achieve her ends.

At Herod's birthday party, where he was surrounded by guests and where the wine would have been flowing, Herodias sent her daughter to dance for the king. We read that,

> "... *the daughter of Herodias danced before them, and pleased Herod. Whereupon he promised with an oath to give her whatsoever she would ask.*"
>
> (MATTHEW 14:6–7)

It was a rash thing to do and Herod played right into Herodias' hands.

> "*And she, being before instructed of her mother, said, Give me here John Baptist's head in a charger. And the king was sorry: nevertheless for the oath's sake, and them which sat with him at meat, he commanded it to be given her. And he sent, and beheaded John in the prison. And his head was brought in a charger, and given to the damsel: and she brought it to her mother.*"
>
> (MATTHEW 14:8–11)

What a terrible commission to be laid on that young girl whose name isn't even mentioned in the scripture. Herodias must have known that if Herod was open to her seduction and would commit a crime as heinous as betraying his brother by sleeping with his wife, then he would be open to the seductive charms of her daughter too. And she was right! Herod promised her anything she wanted and then regretted his actions.

How tragic that Herodias' daughter was drawn into such ungodly practices. And how tragic wherever children have had role models who have modelled seduction and promiscuity to them; role models who have taught by their actions that fornication and adultery are "normal"; fathers who didn't know better who have encouraged their children to follow the way of the world and did nothing to prevent them falling into ungodly, damaging lifestyles. What foolishness on the part of the parents and how sad that a godly pattern was not established to guide them.

TESTIMONIES OF THOSE WHOM GOD HAS HEALED

Despite the absence of godly patterns of behaviour, it never ceases to astonish me how God can heal and restore and put people's lives back together. Through our ministry *Sozo Ministries International* I have had the privilege of ministering to many people who have needed to find resolution and peace with God over their relationship with their father. It has been amazing and awesome to see how God has ministered His healing and brought so many people to a place of wholeness. One lady, Leah, described experiencing a pain in her stomach whenever she spoke about her father. She also suffered from a pain that ran the length of her spine. With insight from the Holy Spirit we were able to identify that this was because her father had been the backbone of her life instead of God. She said that when she surrendered to God and asked Him to be the centre of her life, her circumstances changed completely and she realised that she had been set free from the pain. Here are some other testimonies:

Henry, who attended a Sozo conference, had this to say:

"I honour my father because he was a lovely man, but the penny has finally dropped for me in a big way. The surname I inherited is 'Waylen' because my father was called Waylen, but really I am a son of God. So it might sound silly to say, but in a real sense my surname is 'God' after 'Father God' because I am His son and He is my pattern. It doesn't matter that there were shortfalls in

John Waylen's pattern because I am a son of my Father and He is my pattern now."

Another friend, James, gave the following testimony:

"Like many of us I didn't have the perfect father and I wasn't the perfect son, but just recently God has shown me how much of a barrier that has been to me. I realised that all my life I have felt as though I'm going to get into trouble for something. I bless my dad and I love him and honour him, and I know he had a horrible time as a little boy, but I developed a fear of authority from my dad. And that fear of authority has caused me to be always ducking and diving, keeping out of the reach of authority. I'm fine when I'm on my own, but as soon as I come under someone else's authority I get this feeling: I'd better watch myself and be careful in case I do anything wrong. That has haunted my life and really crushed my spirit.

When I was a young man I had the strength and determination to overcome this thing holding me back and I did some amazing things, but they usually just crumbled in the end because of the faulty foundation I was building my life on. The revelation came for me during a counselling session where someone gave me the following scripture: *'For we are his workmanship, created in Christ Jesus unto good works, which God hath before ordained that we should walk in them'* (Ephesians 2:10). The thing that hit me was that the person said the Hebrew word for 'workmanship' is 'poem'. We are God's poem. I write a lot of lyrics and so I appreciate the fact that it takes a lot of effort to craft good, poetic lyrics; you have to put a lot into it and you do it because you are passionate about it. What hit me was the fact that God was so passionate and inspired about me that He wrote a poem about my life, about all the good works He had prepared for me to do. The enemy had robbed me of enjoying that, but now I know that I can fulfil those good works because I have a Father. I've always known that He loves me, but now I am really receiving that love and living in it. Praise God!"

Paul gave this testimony about having compassion for his father:

"After listening to the teaching at the Sozo conference lots of pieces of my life came together for the first time like a jigsaw puzzle that I can now see quite clearly. I had a problem relationship with my father and I carried that problem around with me for years. Someone prayed with me and told me that I needed to forgive my father in obedience to the Lord. I did forgive him and I thought I was released from that, but still one piece of the puzzle was missing and that was the word 'compassion'. Then, as I thought about it, I realised that, yes, I do have compassion for my father because of his background. He never knew his own father, so how could he know how to be a father to me? In obedience I had forgiven him, but having compassion for him was what really brought me to a place of freedom. After that experience I thought about my father and all I could think of was love, of what a wonderful man he was. I could never have reached that place without showing him godly compassion as well as forgiving him. Rather than looking back at what was and what could have been, I now look forward and think of my heavenly Father and say, 'Lord, I want to run into Your arms.'"

SUMMARY

- The role of a father according to God's Word is to guide and correct his children. If a child is unwilling to listen and for a time follows a path of foolishness a father has to be prepared to accept them back and show unconditional love and forgiveness. Some of us will not have had that kind of relationship with our dad and instead will have felt the weight of his shame and scorn when we made mistakes. Today God can release you from the feelings of guilt and shame you feel.

- Sometimes, despite being given a godly pattern to follow, people choose their own path in life and follow a course of ungodliness which leads to destruction. We can be thankful that though this is the case, God is merciful and forgives all who come to Him in repentance.

- Others have suffered because their parents have demonstrated a very poor life example to them. In the worst cases they have been led to believe that promiscuity and other ungodly behaviour is the accepted norm, causing much emotional damage.

- Despite this, God can bring healing and restoration to us when we surrender ourselves to Him.

— *Prayers* —

A prayer for those who missed out on forgiveness and restoration with their father:

"Father God, I bring my relationship with my father before You now. You know that there were times when I needed my dad to forgive me for acting foolishly and although I was repentant, the unconditional love and forgiveness I needed was not forthcoming. Help me to have compassion on my dad for the way he reacted and to see how he must have been wounded or embarrassed by my actions. I choose to forgive him, Father, with Your help, and I release him in Jesus' name. I pray that where I missed out on reconciliation with my dad You would bring healing and peace to my heart. Where things have been left undone I pray for Your deliverance, healing and restoration in Jesus' name. Amen."

A prayer for those who competed and struggled with their siblings:

"Heavenly Father, I feel my father didn't help solve the problems that arose between me and my siblings. I confess that I often felt like the one who was pushed out and that I was competing for my father's attention. Please set me free from the pain and any unforgiveness concerning my brothers/sisters. Heal us all and help us to enjoy each other in Jesus' name. Amen."

A prayer for those who rebelled against the godly influence of their parents and followed their own path:

"Father, You know that like the sons of Samuel the prophet, although my parents loved You and tried to set a godly pattern for me to follow, I didn't follow it and chose to go my own way instead. I turn my heart to You in repentance and ask for Your forgiveness now in Jesus' name. I seek to honour my parents for following You and for seeking to impart a godly pattern to me. I pray that You would restore all that I have lost through disobedience, in Jesus' name. Amen."

For those people who had negative parental influences, this may have manifested itself in a number of ways. It could be that money was the god in your home resulting in a flawed pattern so that money has become your god too and a stronghold in your life. It could be that you have suffered from sexual bondage resulting from your parents modelling or encouraging sexual promiscuity as you were growing up. However it has been manifest, know that God is able to set you totally free from the ungodly pattern passed on by your parents.

A prayer for those who have come under negative parental influences:

"Father God, thank You that You are the Great Deliverer who can smash every stronghold and break every ungodly pattern of behaviour, however we have come to learn it. I choose to forgive my parents for guiding me or allowing me to go down a road of ungodly behaviour. I pray, Father, that You would deliver and heal me from the negative effects I have suffered as a result and ask that You would reverse those effects in my life now. I thank You that You have cleansed me and I receive Your healing now in Jesus' name. Amen."

ADOPTION
FOR THE
FATHERLESS

WARNINGS AGAINST
CURSING OUR PARENTS

In Proverbs 1:8–9 we read a beautiful description of the reward of obedience to our parents:

"My son, hear the instruction of thy father, and forsake not the law of thy mother: For they shall be an ornament of grace unto thy head, and chains about thy neck."

The Amplified Bible expands on the description of these benefits saying in verse 9,

"For they are a [victor's] chaplet (garland) of grace upon your head and chains and pendants [of gold worn by kings] for your neck."

It's very tempting for us as adults to reject much of what our parents tried to tell us and to write it off as irrelevant. But we need to realise that obedience to our parents' counsel results in victory for us. Not only because we realise later in life that many of the things they said to us made absolute sense! But also simply because God rewards obedience. If we heed our parents' instruction it becomes like a victory garland on our head and we are crowned with God's grace.

Just as there are rewards for obedience in the Bible there are warnings against disobedience and in particular, severe warnings for those who "curse" their parents. In Exodus 21:17 we read that under the Law such an act of shameful disrespect was punishable by death.

"And he that curseth his father, or his mother, shall surely be put to death."

Even though the death penalty of the Old Testament does not apply now because of the grace of Jesus Christ, it still shows us that this was a very serious offence in God's eyes and that it will still carry a penalty, albeit not death. God views speaking words of hate towards our parents extremely seriously, otherwise such a law would never have existed in the first place. And now that we live under grace with the foundation of Old Testament wisdom, we are actually called and equipped by God to surpass the Law. Why is it so serious? Because God knows that cursing our parents, the people who brought us into this world, whose DNA we share, is nothing but a destructive force upon our own lives. In cursing our parents we are effectively cursing ourselves.

Again we read in Leviticus 20:9:

"For every one that curseth his father or his mother shall be surely put to death: he hath cursed his father or his mother; his blood shall be upon him."

And earlier in Exodus 21:15 it says,

"And he that smiteth his father, or his mother, shall be surely put to death."

So God is saying that to curse our parents, or even go so far as to strike one of our parents, puts us on a road to destruction.

Proverbs 20:20 also makes an important comment on this issue:

"Whoso curseth his father or his mother, his lamp shall be put out in obscure darkness."

The Bible says that God's Word is a lamp unto our feet. God's instruction to us is all about light and illumination, spiritual light and discernment. It helps us to see where we need to go, to discern the correct path, to follow the road that leads to life and not death. Here the author of this proverb makes the same point with regard to our parents. Whoever curses their parents (or, we could say, disrespects them, disregards them, refuses to listen to them) is rejecting their counsel and as a result part of their world is plunged into darkness. God says that when we are disobedient we are robbing ourselves.

It is easy to be complacent about such things, despite the seriousness of the warnings in Scripture, and you may think, "Yes, I was a bit rebellious and answered my parents back, but I've moved on now." But whilst I don't want to put anyone under condemnation, some may need to repent of how they handled their relationship with their parents and put things right before God. We looked previously at the issue of provocation, where parents mishandle and frustrate their children, and that may have been an issue for you. But that doesn't mean we are excused to retaliate and disrespect our parents. Examine your own heart before the Lord and see if there is anything which needs to be put right. God can set us free from any bondage relating to a difficult relationship with our parents so that we walk in the light and not in darkness.

ADOPTION FOR THE FATHERLESS

We have looked so far at various aspects of our relationship with our father, but there are still many people who never knew their father at all. There are many who have no real knowledge of either their father or mother, or both, either because they were adopted or because their parents were "absent". This is a devastating situation for anyone to find themselves in, but thank God that He has a special concern for the fatherless. If this applies to you then you are at the top of God's agenda!

God wants us to be adopted into His family for a number of reasons. We will look at each one.

1. *God just wants us in His family*
God promises in Psalm 27:10,

> *"When my father and my mother forsake me, then the LORD will take me up."*

The Amplified Bible puts it this way:

> *"Although my father and my mother have forsaken me, yet the Lord will take me up [adopt me as His child]."*

The good news is that if your parents were not there for you, God wants you to know that you are very much a part of His family because He has adopted you and will take care of you. But it may take a lot of time and healing to really accept and live in that truth.

If your parents were not there for you then you may have had guardians, foster parents or relatives to look after you, somebody who stood in the gap and tried to do their best to raise you, to do what your parents should have done for you. For most people this is a traumatic and isolating experience. Usually people who have suffered from this lack of connectedness to the family have problems with self-worth. Feeling rootless and disconnected touches us deeply and has a profound effect on how we view ourselves and others. Wherever there is a lack of self-worth and value it radiates through the whole of a person's life, especially when it comes to serving alongside others in the Body of Christ, because that person never truly feels "part of the family".

But the truth is, even though other people might reject us, we are never rejected by our Father God. He cares for us, accepts us and adopts us as His beloved children.

Several well known biblical characters were adopted, but one of the most extraordinary images of adoption in the Bible is portrayed through Melchizedek. He is one of the Bible's most mysterious characters and in Hebrews chapter 7 he is referred to as being, *"Without father, without mother, without descent..."* (verse 3). In the Greek the phrase "without descent" means his birth was "unregistered". It was as if he didn't exist because he didn't come from anywhere and then he effectively disappeared. This touched my heart when I studied it recently because it struck me that, actually, it doesn't matter where we've come from, God still wants us in His family. He wants us to be recognised as a part of His great family so that we can belong somewhere, serve alongside everyone else and above all, have our self-worth transformed as we realise how much we are cherished and valued.

If God could bring Melchizedek to the earth without a mother or father and make him a high priest, what have we got to worry about? We have the same heavenly Father. In Scripture Melchizedek is likened to Christ because apparently he has no beginning or end. God put him there and then later took him away. That's hard for us to comprehend, but the fact is, God put us here on this earth, He knows all about us and He has His hand upon us to protect us and guide us because He is our Father. At the end of this section there are some prayers you can pray tailored specifically to those who have trouble accepting that they are adopted into God's family. Pray those prayers and ask God to work in your life, but know that He is so willing to heal you and touch your heart because He wants you to know that you belong to Him.

Remember that Moses, the greatest leader of God's people in the Old Testament, was adopted. He was raised by Pharaoh's daughter. Look at how awesome our God is! He was able to place Moses in the care of the daughter of the very man who was threatening his life, who had promised he would put to death every Hebrew baby. And Moses' sister, Miriam, just happened to be around to get a Hebrew mother to nurse him! God takes care of those He calls to be His own and it is amazing how He does it.

Esther was another child who was adopted. When her parents died she was adopted by her cousin, Mordecai, who raised her as if she was his own daughter. Mordecai later became a courtier of the Persian king, Xerxes, whom Esther later married. She became the queen of Persia, which during her lifetime was the greatest empire in the known world, and interceded on behalf of the Jewish people of the kingdom to prevent their annihilation.

Look at what Esther and Moses achieved even though they were adopted! Why should we allow where we came from and our lack of roots affect us at all? Moses was one of the most amazing leaders in history and Esther one of the most gracious queens. When God takes care of us and adopts us there is no limit to what we can achieve. There is nothing standing in our way.

2. God wants to guide and correct us

God is the perfect example of a model Father to us and because of that He is committed to guiding and correcting us so that we will live a blessed life and not cause harm to ourselves by our actions. Hebrews 12:5–11 describes the process and purpose of God's discipline:

> *"And ye have forgotten the exhortation which speaketh unto you as unto children, My son, despise not thou the chastening of the Lord, nor faint when thou art rebuked of him: For whom the Lord loveth he chasteneth, and scourgeth every son whom he receiveth. If ye endure chastening, God dealeth with you as with sons; for what son is he whom the father chasteneth not? But if ye be without chastisement, whereof all are partakers, then are ye bastards [illegitimate], and not sons. Furthermore we have had fathers of our flesh which corrected us, and we gave them reverence: shall we not much rather be in subjection unto the Father of spirits, and live? For they verily for a few days chastened us after their own pleasure; but he for our profit, that we might be*

partakers of his holiness. Now no chastening for the present seemeth to be joyous, but grievous: nevertheless afterward it yieldeth the peaceable fruit of righteousness unto them which are exercised thereby."

God says that if we are one of His children then He needs to guide us. If we are in relationship with Him there will inevitably be some correction. But it is for our good. The purpose of it is to shape holiness in our lives. God's correction in our lives proves that we are legal sons and daughters of God and we are not illegitimate. Our earthly fathers corrected us and we responded to that, so how much more should we submit to and respect God's correction which will bring life to us?

Correction comes with relationship. The biblical pattern is that fathers have to discipline their sons because it is part of the bonding process. If our father didn't correct us properly then we missed out on the bonding that should have taken place. How much more then do we need to allow our heavenly Father to lovingly correct us and bring direction by His Word so that we are closely bound with Him? If we've got any sense we will submit to our Father's correction because it is intended to release us into blessing. God knows what is best for us. Whenever we decide to reject or try to avoid His correction we effectively remove ourselves from His covering and protection and that is a dangerous place to be.

3. God wants us to be sons not servants
Galatians 4:5–7 says,

> *"To redeem them that were under the law, that we might receive the adoption of sons. And because ye are sons, God hath sent forth the Spirit of his Son into your hearts, crying, Abba, Father. Wherefore thou art no more a servant, but a son; and if a son, then an heir of God through Christ."*

The key word here is "receive". We have to open our hearts to God and be able to receive the free gift of adoption into His family. It is a gift from God to be able to belong. God wants us to realise that we are sons and not servants. We need to become "sons" of God in our hearts. We must not have a slave mentality and neither must we know we are sons and daughters of God purely in our heads. We need to know it in our hearts and live like children of the King. Think about this! It is such a powerful truth. Knowing that we are children of God does so much to set us free from the agony of wondering who our earthly father was, whether we knew him personally or not, whether he had any part in our lives or not. When the revelation hits us that we are here on earth to fulfil a destiny prepared for us by our heavenly Father, it changes everything.

Paul has a lot to say about us being children of God throughout his New Testament writings. In Galatians 3:26–29 he writes,

> *"For ye are all the children of God by faith in Christ Jesus. For as many of you as have been baptized into Christ have put on Christ. There is neither Jew nor Greek, there is neither bond nor free, there is neither male nor female: for ye are all one in Christ Jesus. And if ye be Christ's, then are ye Abraham's seed, and heirs according to the promise."*

We become God's children through faith in Jesus, so if we seek to develop our faith by continually absorbing the truth of God's Word the result will be a greater awareness of our sonship and a more intimate relationship with the Father. Someone might respond to this by saying, "I haven't got much faith, that's why I don't feel close to God" but this is wrong thinking and reveals our tendency to want to have formulas we can refer to so that we can understand our relationship with God in human terms. In fact, faith is a gift that God Himself gives to us. We receive it as a free gift from Him and it grows within us as we read His Word. We just *have* faith because God has given it to us, and because we have faith in Jesus Christ we become children of God.

John 1:12–13 says,

> *"But as many as received him, to them gave he power to become the sons of God, even to them that believe on his name: Which were born, not of blood, nor of the will of the flesh, nor of the will of man, but of God."*

We become sons of God through a spiritual birthing. It doesn't happen through the flesh (i.e. we cannot do anything at all to earn the right), nor by the will of man, but only by God through faith in Christ. What is more it is free and it is available to us now. God is waiting for people to respond to His amazing offer. We have a Father in Heaven! That means we belong.

4. *God wants us to abide in Him and be protected*

As well as recognising that we are His sons and not His slaves, God also wants us to learn to abide in Him, that is, remain in Him and be in His presence constantly, keeping an intimate relationship with Him. That way we will not forget who we are in Christ and begin to doubt our identity.

John 15:9–10 says,

> *"As the Father hath loved me, so have I loved you: continue ye in my love. If ye keep my commandments, ye shall abide in my love; even as I have kept my Father's commandments, and abide in his love."*

Obedience to the Father releases the ability to abide in Him. Abiding means to live somewhere, not just pass through. Because Jesus always obeyed the Father's commandments He lived constantly in His presence and likewise He tells us that if we obey His commandments *we* will live continually in *His* love and care. It is time that we made the decision in our hearts to not just visit God occasionally, but to dwell and abide in Him, to be with Him constantly. Then we will be strong, confident and utterly immoveable in Him. Our self-worth will be transformed as we receive this revelation from God's Word.

So often we look at other people and think, "I don't know God like they do, I don't hear God or feel His presence like they do!" This idea of comparing ourselves to others is one of our greatest problems. The solution is to take our eyes off other people and fix our eyes on Jesus. All the time we are looking at other people and their relationship with God we are missing out ourselves. All we need to know is that if it is written in the Bible then we can have it. We need to pray and ask God to give us a real revelation of what it means to be adopted by Him and then to abide in Him. When we abide in God we will understand Him more and the Word of God will come alive to us.

In the previous section our friend James shared that he was always fearful of people in authority. God is the ultimate authority, but He doesn't want us to be afraid of Him. Having the "fear of the Lord" as Scripture describes is to have an awesome, godly respect for the Lord, but it is not to be afraid of Him like we would be of an earthly father who is not consistent in the way he deals with us. God's authority is something that makes us feel safe, protected and nurtured.

THE ROLE OF GOD'S FAMILY IN ADOPTION

What does it mean in practice to be adopted into God's family? Yes, it means we now have a direct relationship with God the Father through Jesus, but we also have one another – our brothers and sisters in Christ. One of the most amazing things about the Body of Christ that many people miss is the fact that God uses it to provide us with a place of healing, protection and guidance. Remember Jesus' commission to Peter as He appeared to him after His resurrection. Three times He told Peter, "Feed my lambs, feed my sheep..." The Church, the Body of Christ, is the place where we can be fed and nurtured. We each have a responsibility to seek God personally through His Word and prayer, but we also have each other as support. God wants us to enjoy and embrace the accountability that comes from being in fellowship with other believers.

When we are adopted into God's family we suddenly have just that – a huge family! We see this theme running throughout Scripture. Here's Paul speaking to the church at Thessalonica and he says,

> *"As ye know how we exhorted and comforted and charged every one of you, as a father doth his children, that ye would walk worthy of God, who hath called you unto his kingdom and glory. For this cause also thank we God without ceasing, because, when ye received the word of God which ye heard of us, ye received it not as the word of men, but as it is in truth, the word of God, which effectually worketh also in you that believe."*

(1 THESSALONIANS 2:11–13)

Here we see a spiritual father in the Church bringing help to other believers. Paul exhorted his fellow Christians and brought comfort, instructing them as a father would his children to behave appropriately and to walk in godliness. Let's look briefly at what these words mean in the Greek. To "exhort" means to "comfort" and to "invoke" by imploring someone, for instance, to do something. To "comfort" is to "encourage" and to "console". For Paul this would have meant intercession, supplication and prayer, since he could not be with the Thessalonians all the time. He was praying for them to be comforted and encouraged. What a need there is in the Body of Christ for godly people who will pray for others; spiritual fathers and mothers who can bring encouragement and console those who need it. That is wonderful, but there is more than that.

We also read that Paul "charged" the believers to walk worthy of God. This word "charged" has much more forceful connotations. It literally means to flog and scourge with a whip. None of us expect to see people walking around carrying whips in the Church. Not many people would want to join us if we did! So what does Paul mean? He means that along with comfort and encouragement we should expect there to be godly correction in the Church among the believers. All of us need to be able to receive correction and guidance from the godly men and women God has put in place as our leaders. We must view this in the same way that we view correction from the Lord – that it is intended for our good, to help us to reach our destiny in Christ, and to illuminate our path and guide us out of darkness.

There should be a great sense of safety and security in the Body of Christ where we can share things with one another, discuss them and correct each other if necessary. Most of us will have had instances where we believed something to be true and we thought we knew it better than anyone else, but then months or years later we realised that, actually, we don't see things that way at all any more. It is easy to trip up in our beliefs and to drift off course doctrinally, for instance, if we don't expose ourselves to sound Bible teaching or give ourselves the opportunity to run things past other people. This wonderful structure that God has created is there to edify and build us up. We should be able to receive spiritual nourishment, advice, encouragement, consolation, comfort and guidance. This is God's plan for His family.

Another lovely meaning of this word "exhortation" is console which means to alleviate misery or distress of mind. It is a beautiful picture of one person coming alongside another who is perhaps confused or distressed and alleviating their misery with words of strength, comfort and encouragement.

Exhorting is the act of refreshing someone's spirit when they are spiritually dry. God wants us to be able to minister to one another in this way. We need to be whole, healed people so that we can alleviate the suffering of others in the Body.

Ephesians 2:18–22 says,

> *"For through him we both have access by one Spirit unto the Father. Now therefore ye are no more strangers and foreigners, but fellow citizens with the saints, and of the household of God; and are built upon the foundation of the apostles and prophets, Jesus Christ himself being the chief corner stone; in whom all the building fitly framed together groweth unto an holy temple in the Lord: In whom ye also are builded together for an habitation of God through the Spirit."*

What an exciting and beautiful picture of what God is doing through His Body! A large majority have gone through a lot of pain regarding their relationship with their earthly father, but Paul's description here of what God is building makes us feel so secure. This is what the Bible says about you and me: that we are fellow citizens of heaven and we belong in God's household. We are no longer "outsiders" but "insiders". We belong. One of our enemy's greatest ploys is to keep believers on the fringes or even outside of the Body of Christ. He delights in it when people get offended with one another and leave the Church as a result, or when people feel rejected and are afraid to really open themselves up to others.

It is sad when people draw back from the Body and refuse to get involved because of deep hurt. What a tragedy! How much they are missing out. Whenever we feel rejected or get offended by someone we must deal with it. People pay a terrible price for withdrawing and doing their own thing. I have seen it happen to so many people over the years. We need to wake up and realise the gift God has given us in His Body and live it to the full. Instead of complaining about all the things in the Church that we don't like, we need to invest in it, have some stickability, and see what we can put into it rather than what we can take out of it. When we begin to say, "I am going to invest in the life of the Church and the lives of other believers, whatever it costs me," that is so instrumental in us receiving our own healing. When we take our eyes off our own problems and focus on helping others, our situation always improves dramatically.

In life, no one ever got anywhere by not pressing in or by doing things only when they felt like it. A wise quote I once heard says, "Successful people do daily what unsuccessful people do sometimes." Someone else has said, "If we always do what we've always done then we'll always be what we've always been." It's time for change. It's time to begin investing in others so that we move on with God ourselves. Let's get excited about being part of the Body of Christ. Let's shake off the grave clothes and move on!

Recently I attended a weekend course for writers. Although it wasn't a Christian event, and as far as I know none of the other delegates were believers, I seemed to spend the whole weekend nurturing people and some interesting things came out of it. Over dinner one lady told me, "I want to write my life story and I want everybody to know what a rough deal I've had, what a terrible life I've had, and how my grandmother mistreated me..." The course tutor's response to this was interesting. He said, "You will never get anywhere or draw anyone to yourself if you just write about your hurt and put people down. It won't do anybody any good!" I thought at the time, what a good piece of advice that is. When I talked to this lady she actually said, "Somebody told me that I need to see a counsellor" at which point I wanted to duck (it was my weekend off!). But by the end of our time together she was able to say to me, "I am going to write my book, but it's going to be really different now. I'm not going to write with a bitter heart." I encouraged her, "No, share your experience, but write something that will set people free."

Just as no one would want to continue reading a book that was totally negative, neither do people want to listen for very long to a person who is bitter, twisted and screwed up. When we meet people like that, if we are honest, we'd usually prefer to walk the other way. How much better it is when we can build people up and input something positive into their life rather than dumping our baggage on them. This is what the Body of Christ should do for us. God wants us to be built up together and edified in our faith, to share His love with each other and to be conscious of putting issues right when they arise, keeping short accounts with one another so that we can go forward together.

The Body of Christ working together, supporting one another, is the best witness we can possibly give to the world. When things are functioning as they should we can just be ourselves and be confident of who we are in Christ, of who God is to us, supremely confident that He is the One who wants to uphold us and be that Father to us. Then we are able to minister effectively to others and see them blessed and progressing in their faith. As Galatians 6:10 says,

"As we have therefore opportunity, let us do good unto all men, especially unto them who are of the household of faith."

God's family is a special family and we should receive special treatment in it just because we belong to this household of faith. The Church is God's worldwide family. We tend to think of our commitment and involvement only in the context of our local fellowship. As I meet many hundreds of people I am very aware that all is not as it should be and many have withdrawn from local fellowship to protect themselves from error or worldly unbiblical practices etc. It would be my prayer for these children of the Lord to find a loving, biblical place to be fed, nurtured and loved. If this applies to you, my heart goes out to you. When seeking a fellowship to belong to look for the love of Jesus and holiness. Acts 2:41–47 gives us the guidelines for how a godly church should operate.

WE ARE ACCEPTED AND LOVED

I would encourage you to read the whole of Ephesians chapter 1 and to really mediate on the truths it contains. It is a beautiful passage about all the spiritual blessings we have in Christ. I want to bring out just two verses here which say,

"Having predestinated us unto the adoption of children by Jesus Christ to himself, according to the good pleasure of his will, to the praise of the glory of his grace, wherein he hath made us accepted in the beloved."

(EPHESIANS 1:5–6)

The key phrase for us here is *"accepted in the beloved"*. That phrase needs to be a *rhema* word of God to each of us right now, that we are accepted into the family of those who are all called beloved of God. We need to know that's how God sees us: accepted and beloved.

In this verse Paul tells us the amazing truth that not only are we accepted and loved by God, but we were chosen, selected and singled out by Jesus before we were born, before anything ever happened to us. Our chosenness was predetermined and we were ordained to be adopted by God before the beginning of the world. This is an awesome truth that needs to get embedded deep in our souls. Our hearts need to respond to this truth. Today you need to respond by saying, "I belong to God's family and I will deal with every obstacle in my life that would prevent me from enjoying my place in His Body." Determine that whatever it takes you will deal with the hurts of the past, any unforgiveness that is still lurking, any bitterness and regret, and you will pursue healing so that you can become a blessing to others in God's family. Once you make that decision then the love and acceptance of God will begin to permeate your soul.

SUMMARY

- The Bible warns us about the dangers inherent in cursing our parents and refusing to show them respect. God rewards obedience and He rewards us when we are obedient to our parents even though we may not always agree with them. The Bible teaches that we are to honour our parents, but we should not be confused about what this means. God expects us to honour them for their position as our parents. It does not mean that we have to obey them, especially if they are pursuing an ungodly path in life.

- There are people who have no real knowledge of their father either because he was absent during their childhood or because they were adopted from birth. God's heart is always towards the fatherless and He longs to adopt everyone into His family. Psalm 27:10 promises that when our parents forsake us, the Lord will take up our case.

- When God adopts us into His family we receive all the benefits an earthly father could give us, but so much more besides. God will:
  - Guide us and correct us
  - Help us realise we are sons and not servants
  - Teach us to abide in Him so that we are protected
  - When we belong to God's family we not only have God's care and protection, we now belong to a Body of believers and are part of a structure designed by God to feed us, nurture us, encourage us and spur us onward in our journey with Christ.

- Each one of us who puts our faith in Jesus Christ can know and experience the amazing truth that we are called and chosen by Him from before the foundation of the world. We are accepted and loved in God's family, therefore we must decide in our heart to respond to that and pursue our wholeness and healing in Him.

— *Prayers* —

A prayer for those who had/have a difficult relationship with their parents and for whom obedience and honouring their parents is difficult for whatever reason:

"Father God, I bring my relationship with my parents before You now. I know that You don't condemn me in any way, but I bring before You things You have highlighted in my life as I have read this book. I pray that You would forgive me for the times when I have not been respectful or honouring of my parents. Lord, You know the circumstances and You are merciful. I repent of anything I did that ran contrary to Your Word and I ask Your forgiveness. Father, I ask You to break any curse upon my life and to shine the light of Your presence into that dark area of my life. Break the power of my own negative words and actions in the name of Jesus, I pray. Thank You, Father. Amen."

A prayer for those who never really knew their father:

"Heavenly Father, You know that I never really knew my father, but I thank You for the promise of Your Word, that though my parents forsake me, You will take me up. I pray that You would touch and heal the hurt in my soul and release me to receive You as my Father in a new way and with a new depth. I pray that You would release the sorrow and mourning that has been locked up in my soul for so long and restore to me all those years that I feel I have lost. Thank You that You are a wonderful Father and You have called me to be a part of Your amazing family. Thank You that You are blessing me with every spiritual blessing in Christ Jesus. Thank You for the revelation that I am Your child, in Jesus' name. Amen."

Sometimes there can be an unhealthy element of control from our parents that inhibits our progress as a Christian. This is a prayer of release from that ungodly control and an acknowledgement of who you are in Christ:

"Father, I trust You for my healing and for Your ongoing work in my soul. I pray, Father, that You would release me from any unhealthy "soul ties" with my earthly father so that I can be completely free to fully receive You as my heavenly Father. Thank You that You are setting me free and healing me from the effects of any ungodly manipulation and control that existed in my relationship with my parents. I acknowledge before You now and receive in my heart the truth that I am accepted and beloved by You. Thank You, Jesus, that You saw me and my life before the foundation of the world and wanted me to belong to You and to be a part of Your amazing family. I praise You, Lord."

A prayer for those who have trouble accepting that they are adopted into God's family:

"Heavenly Father, I want to walk away from all the insecurities in my soul. I want to be set free from that lifelong fear of not belonging. Help me to trust You that I am a part of the family of God and to truly know that You have adopted me. Help me to unconditionally love Your people as my family, that I may know Your love through them too. Amen."

A prayer towards maturity in Christ:
The Bible says,

"But as many as received him, to them gave he power to become the sons of God, even to them that believe on his name: Which were born, not of blood, nor of the will of the flesh, nor of the will of man, but of God."

(JOHN 1:12–13)

I always say that the "children" of God are the ones who sit down, receive and enjoy their inheritance in God. There is nothing wrong with that at all, but there comes a time when we are no longer simply children of God, but adult sons and daughters. The "sons" of God, therefore, are the ones who stand up and move on in His power. Once we have understood and live in the basics of our faith we are faced with a choice to move on into our sonship and become active in our Father's kingdom. There is a time to receive and a time to give out, a time to grow up and move on. If you feel ready to do that, pray the following prayer:

"Father, I no longer want to be just a child, I want to be a son of God. According to Your Word You will give me the power to become what You have destined me to be in Christ. Just as You have set me free, help me to move on in Your power, confident of my relationship with You, knowing that whatever challenges I face You are there with me to see me through. I pray that I would no longer be held back from accomplishing great things for You either by people or circumstances or my own disobedience. I leave behind now everything that has hindered me and choose to move forward with You. Anoint me, Father, to touch this world for Jesus. I receive Your power to function as a son of God in Your kingdom, in Jesus' name. Amen."

About the Author

Marion Daniel came to Christ in the 1970s after a marriage break up and was miraculously healed of spondylosis of the spine. In the early 1980s she heard the message that "God wants you whole" and felt this was key to her receiving her miracle. She has since taken this message from the Bible to everyone who wants to hear and experience wholeness through Jesus.

In 1983 Sozo Ministries International, a healing/deliverance ministry, was birthed and decades later Marion still preaches the wholeness message. She has nine of her family working alongside her and a ministry team of people whose lives have been transformed with the message of healing and wholeness.

About Sozo

www.sozo.org is a regularly updated website that will help you find out all that is going on within the ministry and what we are doing for God. Information on events, meetings and conferences are all available online as well as news sheets, free mp3 downloads and special features. Our miracle testimony section will also stir your soul! Jesus does and will heal today. The testimonies are from real people who all reached out and trusted God.

www.sozobooks.com is the bookshop and resource centre for the ministry. You will find a huge choice of books, including many titles that are unavailable in many Christian bookstores, as well as Marion's teachings on DVD, CD, mp3 and audio cassette.

If this book has been helpful the following audio messages would complement this theme:

Sets
Forgiving Is for Giving
Conquering Relationships
Rejection Hurts

Single messages
The Father Heart of God
Barriers to Father God
Gift of a Godly Father
Barriers to God's Love

See our media catalogue for more...

We hope you enjoyed reading this New Wine book.
For details of other New Wine books
and a range of 2,000 titles from other
Word and Spirit publishers visit our website:
www.newwineministries.co.uk
email: newwine@xalt.co.uk